Ultimate Guide to e-Cigarette Retail Business

Step By Step Guide on how to Open a Vape Shop on a Budget

By

Shane H. Alexander

Published by:

CSB Academy

CSB Academy Publishing Co.

P.O. Box 966

Semmes, Alabama 36575

Cover and interior design by: Angela Anderson

Introduction...7

What Is The e-Cigarette? 8

Who Makes Them?...10

Why the e-Cigarette Retail Business?...............11

How Much Money Do I Need to Start It? 11

How Much Money Can I Make? 12

How Do I Start?...15

How Do You Allocate the Budget of $20,000? 16

Part One: Opening the Brick and Mortar Store 17

Step 1: Site Selections and Leasing a Storefront: 17

Visibility from the Road 17

Store Size 17

Negotiate the Lease.....................................17

Step 2: Leasehold Improvements and Decorations........20

Choose the Right Name for Your Store.........20

Have the Exterior Sign Made and Placed.......22

Set Up Display and Showcases 22

Step 3: Product Ordering and Shipping 24

Ordering Inventory 24

Paying for Products......................................26

Step 4: Pre-Opening Marketing Plan 28

Branding Your Store.....................................29

Local Promotions 29

Promotional Materials.................................29

Set Greeting Procedures..............................30

On-Site Advertising 30

Local Media 30

Step 5: Merchandising the Store 31

    Front Door Placement 31

    Highlight Desires...31

    Lighting 32

    Showcase Groups of Items 32

    Add an Unrelated Item 32

    Add Signs 32

    Move Sale Items to the Back 33

    Change Displays Often..33

    Get Customer Opinions 33

    Know Your Hottest Selling Products 34

Step 6: Grand Opening 34

    Greet Every Customer at the Door 34

    Give Out Goodies..35

    Provide Entertainment 36

    Introduce Your Products...36

    Offer Information Packets 36

Step 7: Operating Your Store..37

    Choosing Cash Registers 37

    Choosing PC's..39

    Choosing Software..41

    Keeping Track of Inventory..43

    Setting Store Hours..44

    Post-Opening Glitches and Issues:...............................44

Step 8: Post-Opening Marketing 47

    Ongoing Marketing..48

    Calendar-Centered Promotions.....................................48

    Seasonal Promotions 49

    Email Marketing...49

  Step 9: How to Wholesale to Other Local Retailers.....................50

    Approach Gas Station Owners.................................50

    Offer to Supply Basic E-Cig Line 51

    Provide Promotional Materials...............................51

    Get There First 51

Part Two: Opening the e-Commerce Store 52

  Step 1: Domain Registration and e-Commerce Hosting 52

  Domain Registration 52

  e-Commerce Hosting 54

    Shopping Cart Elite 55

  Step 2: Finding a CC Processor 56

    Flagship Merchant Services 56

    CreditCardProcessing.com..................................57

    Volusion 57

    Leaders 57

  Step 3: Building Your e-Store.......................................57

    How to Build the e-Store 58

    Templates 58

    Organize..58

    Products..58

    Payment Processing..59

    Tax Rate 59

    Shipping 59

    Other Pages 59

    Meeting Basic e-Commerce Site Requirements 59

Hiring a Virtual Assistant 60

Step 4: Merchandising Your e-Store 61

Featured Items 61

Similar or Related Products 61

Site Search 61

Step 5: Opening Your e-Store 62

Press Releases 62

Step 6: Promoting Your e-Store 66

How to Rank on Search Engines 66

Become a Social Media Expert 70

Put Out Coupon Codes 71

Cross Promotion with Offline Store 73

The Last Word 75

Appendix 1A: List of Reputable e-Cigarette Manufacturers 76

Appendix 1B: E-Liquid Sources 78

Quality: 78

Shipping Expense: 78

Exceptions to the Rule: 78

U.S. e-Liquid Manufacturers 79

Points to Remember about e-Liquid for Resale 79

Appendix 2: Basic Standard Order Sheet Examples 81

Appendix 3: Sample Promotional Materials 86

We Carry Full Line of Premium Electronic Cigarettes and Accessories
....87

Appendix 4: Basic Information Handouts to Customer 88

Introduction

It was just a few years ago that I started using the e-cigarette. I had been smoking combustible cigarettes for a long time. When I had to have throat surgery, my doctor warned me that I must not smoke for the week of the surgery. I was devastated. An entire week! I knew I wanted to come up with an alternative way to get the nicotine and have that pleasurable experience. Several friends used e-cigarettes. They told me how much they enjoyed vaping and explained what they knew about the health factors involved. I decided to investigate further. I started by doing hours of research online. I liked what I read and decided to try the e-cigarette.

Once I tried the e-cig, I knew I could give up smoking combustible cigarettes for good. The e-cig vapor gave a crisper, cleaner taste. Interested in learning more, I looked online for more information on the product and found out how to make my own e-juice flavors. I experimented until I had the exact taste I liked and the nicotine strength that suited me. After I discovered the e-cig, I could vape at home and even in public without fear. If someone had never seen an e-cigarette before, I simply explained to them what it was. They always seemed happy for the information and glad that I was not filling the room with noxious smoke.

As a satisfied customer of the e-cigarette, I could not wait to share my newfound pleasure with others. I wanted to start a business at the time, so I decided to try selling the e-cigarette. I had read the statistics about how fast this business was growing, so I expected to do well. In fact, the business took off even faster than I had dreamed. I consider it one of my greatest successes. I want to share my thoughts and experiences on e-cigarette retail business so you can start a booming business like I have. Keep reading to find out what an e-cig is, why they are so popular, and how I put together the brick and mortar stores as well as my e-commerce site.

What Is The e-Cigarette?

The "e" in e-cigarette stands for "electronic," referring to the technology that drives the e-cig. The e-cigarette is a newer, and in my opinion better, version of the classic tobacco cigarette. Instead of inhaling smoke that is filled with cancer-causing substances like tar and up to thousands of other harmful chemicals, you puff a clean, odorless vapor. The e-cigarette can contain nicotine if you prefer, in doses up to 24mg. However, you do not have to use nicotine if you choose not to have it.

Many people use these devices to quit smoking combustible cigarettes for health or social reasons. They are an inexpensive alternative to smoking at about one-third the cost, which is one reason the market is simply exploding.

The e-cigarette usually takes the form of a plastic tube, or is designed to look just like a traditional cigarette, cigar or pipe. There are several parts to the e-cigarette. The microprocessor of the device sends a signal to the ion battery as soon as you draw in air across it. Then, the atomizer produces a vapor that contains nicotine and/or other simple ingredients from the e-juice cartridge.

One excellent property of the e-cigarette is that you can get prefilled cartridges or fill them yourself to contain an almost endless variety of e-juice flavors. You can stick with traditional tobacco cigarette flavors, or you can experiment with flavors like banana, coconut, rum and coke, chocolate, and the list goes on and on.

The e-cigarette business has thrived since it started. Last year, net sales were in the low $100 millions, while this year, market experts predict that net sales will reach as high as $1.7 billion. By 2015, the market will still be expanding, with net sales over $3 billion expected.

Yet the business is still in its infancy. There is incredible potential for expansion, especially right now. Those same market professionals also believe that the market will continue to expand, with e-cigs outselling traditional cigarettes by 2047. Does this sound like the kind of opportunity you are looking for? If so, you have company and wealthy company at that.

The three biggest tobacco companies are pushing to take over the e-cigarette market as fast as they can. They recognize that consumers worldwide are tired of paying extremely high prices for cartons or packs of combustible cigarettes. They realize that cigarettes have been incontrovertibly proven to damage the lungs and cause cancer. They see e-cigarettes as a way to refocus their current product line so that it takes these facts into account. They are smart – they want a piece of this pie, and they want a huge piece of it at that.

The e-cigarette is not intensely regulated at this point, which makes it easier and less expensive to sell than it might be later. Currently, the FDA places propylene glycol, one of the primary ingredients of the e-juice, on their list of substances that are generally recognized as safe. So far, the agency neither promotes nor discourages use of e-cigarettes. However, recently the FDA has been under pressure to label them as unsafe. Does this mean the e-cig is actually harmful? No, what it means is that makers of nicotine replacement therapy products like patches, gums and pills do not want to lose business to the e-cig.

Actually, at the time of this writing, the FDA is working with e-cigarette manufacturers to standardize the industry. They are always concerned about public health, of course. At the present time, it seems that the FDA is moving toward allowing the sale of the e-cig provided that the agency can regulate the product to their satisfaction.

All these factors explain why this moment, right now, is the optimal time to get in on the e-cigarette retail business.

Who Makes Them?

E-Cigarettes were first made in China. So far, this tradition continues, as 85% e-cigs are still handmade in that country. The e-juice, the liquid that is used to produce the vapor, sometimes comes from the U.S. and other countries, but the e-cig itself is still made mostly in China.

The first e-cig was offered in 2004 after a Chinese pharmacist named Hon Lik created the device in 2003. The patent was granted in 2007. Already millions of people worldwide have switched from traditional tobacco cigarettes to the new electronic cigarette.

As of this writing, over 1000 companies exist for the sole purpose of making e-cigarettes and the accessories that go with them. In each of those companies, anywhere from 300 to 1000 workers in two or three shifts are busy making these devices every day. The good news for you if you are considering entering the e-cig retail business, is that the e-cigarettes they make are selling fast enough to keep these workers very busy. The industry is taking off like wildfire.

Why the e-Cigarette Retail Business?

Previously in this book, I talked about how fast the industry is growing. Since you have read this far, it is likely that you are starting to seriously consider starting your own e-cig store. Why is the e-cigarette retail business to appealing? The answer is simple. E-cigarettes present an untapped market where you can not only have a business, but also expand it around the corner, around the Internet, and ultimately, around the world.

By starting an e-cigarette business now, you can get into the market before it becomes saturated. Too many products are hard to sell. You have to take a low profit margin on those other products because everyone else is trying to sell the same thing. The demand is great, but the supply is even greater.

And think about this: what else would you sell if you do not sell e-cigarettes? This is the product that will change the way people think about cigarettes. Just try to come up with any other item you could sell that is in the position e-cigs are now. The demand is growing exponentially, and retailers have not yet caught up with it. People are excited about the product, and large companies are, too. The time for e-cig retail is here.

How Much Money Do I Need to Start It?

Like any other business, there is no limit to the amount of money you can invest in setting up your e-cig retail store. Even if you start moderately, you need money for display cases, shelving, cash registers, store decorations and do not forget the initial e-cig inventory.

Startup costs for an e-cigarette business vary widely for two main reasons. First, the amount you have to pay to lease a storefront depends on the real estate prices for the area. For example, to lease the storefront you need in New York City would cost you about ten times the cost for one in a smaller town like Peoria, Illinois. Because of this, I suggest that you choose a location in a small town or suburb. That way you will have less competition and a better customer base for your store.

The second reason for variation in startup costs for an e-cig retail business is that tastes and pocketbooks vary. If you have the capital for a larger, more lavish store, you might choose to spend more money on display cases, inventory and decorations. That is entirely up to you.

However, in this book, I will focus on a moderate-sized business so that you can take advantage of the opportunity even if you are not wealthy. I shoot for a budget of around $20,000. I have actually done this myself. I set up two stores, each with initial costs under $20,000. That provides enough money to set up a nice storefront and have an adequate amount of inventory to serve the customers in nearly any small town you choose.

How Much Money Can I Make?

Every store is different. Profits depend on several factors including the location and demographics of the area surrounding the store. You have to carefully research and analyze these factors to get a solid idea of how much product your unique store will sell.

In this book, I will focus on my own successful experiences to give you a basic understanding of how great the potential is in this retail business. Consider an e-cig store that I own and operate. This store turns a profit of 100% to 300%. That is not a misprint. Yes, our return on investment is up to 300%! And that is return on investment, not markup!

If you are new to the business world, you might not know the difference between these three terms: markup, profit margin and ROI. Before I go any further, let me take a moment and explain the difference.

Markup is the mathematical difference between the cost you pay to the supplier of the product and the amount you sell it for in your store. For example, you might pay $1 for a product and sell it for $2. The markup in this instance is 100%. Yet this does not include your business costs. Somehow, you have to pay to keep your store open and running smoothly and not eat away the amount you gained by the markup.

Profit margin, on the other hand, is a ratio based on your net profit divided by your sales x 100. Does that sound complicated? It is really very simple. The profit margin is a percentage describing the profit you gained– after paying for the product, international shipping, taxes, etc. – divided by the dollar amount of the products you sold.

The most exciting figure is called Return on Investment (ROI). The ROI is figured as (sales-cost)/cost. The ROI is a percentage based on the amount you gain from the investment you make. For example, say your purchase price plus expenses is $2. If you sell it for $4, your ROI would be calculated like this: ($4-$2)/$2. Multiply this by 100 to get the percent. The resulting number is 200, which translates to a 200% return on your investment! And this figure, unlike the markup, takes into account all your costs for the product.

Let me tell you about my own experiences with wholesale vs. retail in my store. One of the products we sell is an Ego style rechargeable single e-cigarette kit with a USB charger. We sell it for $24.99 but our cost for that kit is only $8.50. The profit margin is (24.99 -8.5)/24.99, or 66% profit margin. The ROI is (24.99-8.5)/8.5. This amounts to a 194% return on your total investment.

We also have a very hot-selling item in our store called the Evod atomizer. Atomizers are big sellers in general, and this one is no exception. We sell them easily at a price of $7.99, and our cost is only $2.00, a profit margin of 75%. The ROI on this item is 300%!

The product that sells more than any other in an e-cigarette store is the e-liquid. Our price is $4.99 to $7.99 for a 10 ml bottle. Yet it only costs us around $1.75 for each bottle. That's 65% profit margin for the $4.99 bottle and 78% for the $7.99 bottle. The ROI for the $4.99 bottle is 185%, while the ROI for the $7.99 bottle is a whopping 357%! Does that sound like a good profit to you? If it does, then you will be even happier when you own ROI reaches over 300%! In each of these examples I have taken into account everything it takes to carry the product in my store. I even included the cost for all international shipping and payment system fees.

If you follow the instructions in this guide, use good marketing strategies, and price the products according to the advice I give here, your sales should be anywhere from $3500 to $7000 per week.

Let us go back to my experience with my first store. The very first week, we did not get all the marketing done in time. Specifically, we were late in sending out the sales flyers. Yet even that week, we still sold $4,300 worth of products. Once we followed through with all our marketing plans, our store never did less than $6,500 in sales per week from the 3rd week on.

To figure my profit from these sales, simply subtract fixed and variable costs from the sale price. As you do the math, remember to include expenses like rent, utilities and other costs of doing business. If you do the calculations carefully, you can easily see that I make an impressive profit my store. Now here is the great news: You can have the same range of profits if you pay special attention to my advice in this guide.

How Do I Start?

The hardest part of opening up an e-cigarette store is deciding whether to do it or not. The process of starting the business is simple as long as you follow a suitable step-by-step process. The most important thing you can do before you begin is to make a solid commitment to your new business.

Once you decide to begin, start by finding a funding source. If you are borrowing the money, choose your lender carefully. Shop banks and other lenders to get the best interest rate you can and be sure to read the fine print of any contract before you sign it.

Next, if you have a full-time job, figure out how you will make time for your store. This especially important as you set up and begin operations.

Now you are ready to decide where to set up your store. Look for a location in a middle class neighborhood. Study the demographics of each location you consider. The best locations are towns with plenty of people within your target market. These people include 30- to 50-year-old men and women with a median annual household income of $25,000 to $75,000.

Once you have researched and studied the demographics of the general area, narrow your choices even further by eliminating the parts of town that do not meet the criteria for age and income of most residents.

How Do You Allocate the Budget of $20,000?

Every location and store are different, so let me just tell you how I allocated my funds for my first store. The first item on my list was the store lease, including first and last month's rent. That was $1500 to start and then $750 each month after that. I spent $2247 on store improvements. After that, I set aside enough money to buy the starting inventory. At that point, I had met the most basic physical requirements for the store and I was ready to proceed with doing the work to open it.

Now are you ready to learn how to run your e-cigarette retail store? The incentives are tremendous. You get to bring a wildly popular product into a new area, the profit margins are excellent, the startup costs are very low compared to other retail businesses, and you have all the information in this guide to get started. Read on to Part 1 for advice on opening a brick and mortar store and Part 2 for information on how to go global by putting an e-commerce site online.

Part One: Opening the Brick and Mortar Store

The e-cigarette business described in this book is actually two businesses in one. You can open both a brick and mortar store and an online store. Before I get to the e-commerce store, we will talk first about opening that brick and mortar store. Here are the steps you need to take:

Step 1: Site Selections and Leasing a Storefront:

There are several factors you need to consider when selecting the site for your storefront. Here are a few things to think about:

Visibility from the Road

Despite all the marketing you will do, you cannot make much profit if your customers cannot find you. When you consider a site, drive to it. The first time you go there, notice whether it is easy to spot as you drive toward it. Your future customers will be looking for that storefront, too. Make sure they can see it when they get there.

Store Size

Look for a store that is in the neighborhood of 1200 square feet. This will be plenty large enough to display your merchandise with room for the customers as well. For now, do not lease a large store or you will waste money unnecessarily. Keep your costs low with a right-sized store.

Negotiate the Lease

After you settle on a storefront you would like to use for your e-cigarette retail business, it is time to negotiate the price and conditions of the lease. Even if this property is your best option, you still want the best terms possible. So, as you enter negotiations, keep in mind the fact that you are offering to do the landlord a favor by leasing the property. Here are some tips to help you succeed.

- Compare Lease Prices Before You Approach the Landlord

- Investigate the amount you will pay for a similar property to the one you are considering. You can do this easily online through sites like loopnet.com. The Loop net site and service offers a vast store of information including statistics on local lease property. This property is generally priced by the square foot, and Loop net shows this figure as a part of each listing. Go in knowing the price range you should expect, and negotiate if necessary to keep the lease payment within that range.

- Deal with the Landlord Directly

  A landlord's broker represents the landlord's interests. Yet you are more likely to get a favorable outcome if you deal with the landlord directly. The broker is trying to get the most money from you that he can get. The landlord usually is just trying to fill a vacancy and is more willing to make concessions in most cases.

- Find Out What the Lease Payment Covers

- Sometimes the rent you pay each month covers items like utilities, janitorial services, maintenance, property tax, insurance and parking. When you negotiate the lease, do not assume that any of this is included in the rent. Ask about all of it. Then, if one of these items is not paid for by the landlord, ask the landlord to drop the rent if it is too high for you to cover them within your $20,000 budget.

- Demand an Out

  One important thing to have in a lease is a way to get out of it if you need to make changes. There are several reasons you might need a bigger or smaller store. The neighborhood might change over time, and you might need to relocate to follow your target market. Whatever the reason, you need to have the option to end the lease if you choose.

- Ask for a Lease Raise Cap

  Most lease agreements start out with a clause for raising your rent, usually on an annual basis. The landlord might be willing to drop this clause if you argue your case well. However, if you cannot get him to drop the annual rent raise from the contract, try asking for a cap on the allowed raise. This ensures that you will still have a reasonable rent payment for the term of the lease.

- Know a Typical Lease Agreement When You See It

- A typical commercial lease is quite different from a residential lease. For one thing, landlords use their own customized forms rather than relying on standard forms. Most leases are written for years. The document includes the terms and conditions of the lease. It should specify exactly what space you are paying for, the cost of the rent including increases, and the services that are provided for the leased property. There are usually clauses that limit your use of the property, including where you can place signs. Look for an option to renew the lease if you so choose.

- Know If the Property Is Fully Constructed

    Look carefully at the property before you sign the lease. Make sure that all construction is complete. The walls, floors, lighting AC and heating are in place and fully functional.

Step 2: Leasehold Improvements and Decorations

Once you have leased the property, the next step is to set up your store and prepare it for opening day. Start by improving the property and decorating it the way you choose. Here are some tips to get you started:

Choose the Right Name for Your Store

Before you can set up your store, you need a name for your business. Choose the right name to make your store easier to remember. This is how you go about choosing the perfect name:

- Make It Catchy

    Choose a name potential customers will respond to immediately. People who hear a catchy name like the way it sounds and enjoy repeating the word to others. Make your e-cigarette retail business name catchy, and news of your store will spread like wildfire.

- Make It Brand-able

An ideal name for a business defines your brand. It is not only descriptive of your brand in some way, but it is also unique to your brand. If you want to use a common word, add something to it to make it your own. A good example of this is eTrade.

- Make It Future-Friendly

  Select a name that can work for your business for the long haul. Avoid names that refer to current fads. Think of how your business might expand in the future. Choose a name that can grow with you.

- Check for a Matching Domain Name

  Since the business will eventually include an e-commerce store, you need a brand name that you can match to a domain name. Doing so allows your customers to find you easily on the web. It also makes it easier for potential customers to find you through search.

  For best results in search, choose a name that includes one or two keywords related to your business. In the case of an e-cigarette business, try to incorporate words like "e-cigarette," "e-cig," "vape," or "e-juice."

  Before you choose the name for your business, investigate domain names. If you find one you like, reserve it now so you can build your e-commerce site there later. Until you get your e-commerce site going, you can use the domain for a simple website that gives hours, location and other basic information.

- Claim the Name – Have your new e-cigarette retail store name trademarked. Apply for an LLC and a business license under that name.

Once you choose a name, hire a graphic designer to create a logo using the name. Since you are trying to keep costs down, consider hiring a freelance graphic designer rather than a large design company. Ask to see work samples before you decide who to hire. Be sure to hire on the basis that you must approve the work before you make payment.

Have the Exterior Sign Made and Placed

Contract with a sign maker who can create an appealing exterior sign for your shop. The sign needs to be large enough to attract attention from the road. It needs to display your logo and business name in readable letters.

Finally your sign needs to be visible during all store hours. So, if your store stays open after dark, have the contractor make a lighted sign. When your sign is made up, have it placed somewhere outside your store or in the window where it can make an impression on passersby and direct customers inside.

Set Up Display and Showcases

Like any other store, your e-cigarette retail store needs showcases and displays to highlight the products you sell. You can make them yourself to cut costs, or you can look for great deals on new ones or used ones in good condition.

- Make Them Yourself

  One way to make your own showcases is to look for plans online or in your local library. Examine the plans as closely as possible before you buy them or check them out from the library. Make sure they have a parts list and detailed instructions on how to build.

  If you are an experienced woodworker, another method for you is to go to a store that sells the type of showcases you want to use. Look at them carefully, take measurements and make notes of the parts you need to build them. When you get home, make a simple drawing of the showcase. Then, use your knowhow to construct the displays.

  Always remember that products in the e-cigarette line are very vulnerable to theft. They are small and can be picked up quickly and discreetly. So, you need to have locking showcases. If you make them yourself, buy the locks and install them before you set them out on the floor.

- Buy Them Inexpensively

  You can buy showcases and displays inexpensively if you take the time to find the best deals. First, do some research to find out what you would have to pay to buy new, full-price showcases that would serve your purpose.

  Stores that are going out of business may have display cases they want to sell cheap. Watch the news for businesses that are going into bankruptcy.

If you know the store or believe the business might use display cases that are similar to the ones you want, approach the owner and offer to buy them at a discounted rate.

You can also find good deals from online stores, but make sure you know the total cost including shipping and handling before you order. Compare this total cost to the price you would pay for the displays locally.

- Place Them for Maximum Effect

Once you have the showcases and displays for your store, place them carefully so people can see them easily as they walk through the store Place your most expensive items in a prominent location. Set a display case near the cash register to hold items that encourage customers to buy on impulse. Interesting accessories and novelty e-juice flavors do well in a location like this.

Step 3: Product Ordering and Shipping

At this point, your store is ready to go. Now you need to acquire the initial inventory. Getting the right products to sell is one of your most crucial tasks. Then, you need to order them and have them shipped. I have included some advice and instructions below for this part of your e-cigarette retail business startup process.

Ordering Inventory

Ordering the right inventory for your e-cig retail store is a crucial task. If you do not choose wisely, customers complain and often do not return to the store. In addition, you might encounter legal problems if you sell a product that has harmful ingredients or too much nicotine. On the other hand, when carefully choose only the best products to sell, these problems are diminished or go away completely. Here is a bit of advice on how to stock your store.

- Who to Order From

  Order from suppliers who have been in the e-cig game long enough to establish a solid reputation. When you find a few good vendor, continue to use them regardless of the tantalizing offers you get from newcomers. Find what is best and stick with vendors you know as much as possible. Appendix 1 lists my favorite suppliers. These four companies have proven to be reliable sources of e-cigs, e-juice and related products.

- Suppliers to Avoid

  I suggest you avoid buying e-cig products directly from a Chinese manufacturer. You can find a few great Chinese suppliers, but the search can be costly and time-consuming. Among other manufacturers, the ones that have been around longer than others are more likely to offer satisfactory products, so stay away from most new companies.

- Variations in Quality
  Be aware that the variation in quality among e-cigarettes can be substantial. The problem is mainly in cartridge liquid. A UK government test showed that the contents of the cartridges varied as

much as 23% between batches and as much as 20% even among cartridges from the same batch.

The level of nicotine also proved to be inconsistent, with as much as 83% variation between e-cig cartridges. The level when used, however, did not vary as much as expected because some cartridges were specifically made to deliver more nicotine in the vapor.

Standards and regulations are virtually nonexistent for e-cigarettes and e-cig cartridge content. What does this all mean for you? First, you have to be careful of your suppliers and search for statistics on their products. Second, you can be sure that regulation will eventually happen.

Paying for Products

Paying for e-cigarettes and related products is risky business if you are not careful. Choosing companies listed on Alibaba.com or other sites you find through a search engine is not a wise way to do business. In fact, it is always best to avoid sending out payments to manufacturers you are not familiar with in some way.

In Appendix 1, I have listed reputable suppliers, and I suggest you work with these companies. I have either had an ongoing business relationship with them or visited their factories or both. To keep up with my current best picks, you can also visit my website at http://bestelectroniccigarettehq.com for my most up-to-date list.

Another option is to place your order with me, as I am a direct importer of e-cigarette products. I save on shipping by placing large orders and having them shipped by air instead of using FedEx or UPS. You can find all the information you need to get started on my website, including my list of suppliers and the products I offer.

Even when you know you are doing business with a trustworthy client, you still need to ensure that you choose a reliable payment method. Here are some tips on paying for e-cig products for your retail business.

How to Pay

Never pay without first receiving a Payment Invoice from the supplier. First, place an order with them, identifying all the products you want to buy and the quantity of each item. The company sends you a PI with the price for each item you chose plus the shipping cost and bank fees, also called TT fees. Check out the invoice and make sure everything is listed according to the way you ordered it. Once you approve the PI, then and only then is it time to send the money.

What Is Secure Pay?

To pay securely, wire funds directly to a bank in Hong Kong. At that time, notify the company that you have made the transfer. After another 10-14 days, you receive your shipment of e-cig products. Paying by secure wire transfer from bank to bank is the most secure way to pay.

What Is Not Secure Pay?

Debit cards, checks, credit cards and even some payment sites that most people trust for online business are not necessarily safe. Even if you pay bank to bank, there is a small risk that cybercriminals can strike. The difference is that with bank to bank transfers, the bank is responsible to pay for these problems immediately. With other forms of payment, you can waste a lot of time waiting for these problems to be fixed, or even lose your money with no real hope of recovery. Take my advice and make security the banks' job.

Estimated Transit Time

As you plan your Grand Opening, you need to know how long it will take to receive the products. In most cases, products arrive within 10 to 14 days after you wire the funds to pay for your order. Note the estimated arrival time from the supplier website, or if none is given, ask a customer representative. Whatever estimate you use, your product does not always arrive on the date you expect. So, leave enough time to get the product in before you plan to open the store.

Shipping Cost

Know your shipping costs before you complete your order. You can use this information to shop for the lowest shipping, or use the data to make financial decisions based on your projected profit margins. As a general rule of thumb, shipping costs are about 15-20% of the total cost of products.

Step 4: Pre-Opening Marketing Plan

Start planning your marketing as soon as possible. In fact, begin thinking about how you will market your store as soon as you make the decision to have an e-cigarette retail business. Specifically, you need to think about how you want to brand your store and where and how you want to publicize it.

Branding Your Store

What do you want your e-cig store to be known for in the community? You can focus on the people in your neighborhood who are still smoking or have recently quit by building a reputation for having popular tobacco flavors. Another option is to be the e-cig retailer with the widest variety of e-juice flavors. Or, choose to focus your marketing on luxury at an affordable price. If you market your brand successfully, people will know what you stand for every time they hear or see your name.

Local Promotions

Plan ways to promote your store locally. Look at a calendar of area events to find fairs, concerts and conventions where you can introduce your products and market your store. Make a list of all events you want to attend and investigate the costs and rules for having a concession there.

Promotional Materials

Choose the promotional materials you want to give away or sell to promote your business. You can have your logo put on flyers, posters, brochures. Hand them out directly to people in the neighborhood, put them under windshield wipers at a shopping mall, or send them in the mail. Your flyers need not be big-ticket items. Have a simple flyer made up displaying your logo and the date you are opening. Be sure to include brand messages that tell what makes your store unique.

You can also select wearable advertising like t-shirts, hats and bandanas. Find suppliers who make these products and inquire about price, shipping costs and delivery time. Read reviews of these suppliers to make sure you present the most positive image. Place your order so they will be ready before the grand opening.

Set Greeting Procedures

In this phase of planning, decide how you will interact with customers when they come into your store. What will be your standard greeting? How will you answer the phone? What will you say when they make a purchase and when they leave? These small details are important because the way you treat customers is one way they will remember you. If you have a unique greeting, you can use it in your promotional materials, as well.

On-Site Advertising

Plan how to make people aware that your site will soon be an e-cigarette retail store. You can place "Opening Soon" signs in your store window or in front of your building. Brainstorm for additional ways to promote your store right on the site. For example, you can place a coupon in the local paper for people to come to your site and get a free t-shirt. This on-site event serves two purposes. First, it brings people to your location, often for the first time. Second, when people wear the shirts, others will take notice and ask about your store. And all this takes place before you even open your doors!

Local Media

Decide how to use local media to get the word out for your grand opening. Approach news outlets and offer to give an insider's perspective on e-cigarettes. Know your products thoroughly and become a local expert. Think of ways to be in the news in a positive way without paying for advertising.

Also, decide what local advertising you want to purchase. Television and radio ads are expensive, but see if you can work a few into your budget for the grand opening. Newspaper ads are less costly. However, fewer and fewer people buy a paper version. Ask if there is separate pricing for the online newspaper and decide whether to do both online and offline or just one.

With all your plans in place, it is now time to prepare your store for the grand opening. Set your pre-opening plans aside for a few days if possible so you can concentrate on setting up the store. Soon you will be open for business. Be sure you are ready when the customers arrive.

Step 5: Merchandising the Store

Merchandising refers to anything you do in your store to get people to purchase your product. The most basic merchandising is the way you display your products within your store. Before your grand opening, you need to have your showcases and displays in place. Make the displays appealing to the customers and locate them strategically around your store. Here are a few tips to merchandise your store successfully.

Front Door Placement

Put those products that are newest, most expensive and most desirable nearest to the door of your store. People will see them first as they come in, focusing their attention on the most glamorous products. They also see these items as they are going out the door, enticing them to stay just a little longer to see this new and/or wonderful item.

Highlight Desires

Consumers usually come into a store for the things they need. However, when they see something they really want, a good display leads them to consider spending the extra money. Put your standard, basic and more common items in a low-profile place. Your special items belong in the spotlight.

Lighting

Light up your display so it is easy to see and more attractive. Lighting is especially important with e-cig lines. Many of the products are dark in color, and the majority of items you sell in an e-cigarette retail store are small.

Showcase Groups of Items

As you set up your displays, place items that belong in a group in a single showcase. For example, you could put an e-cigarette, an e-cigarette cartridge, a bottle of e-juice in one display. Place the rest of your inventory in shelves below the display case or behind the counter.

There is no point in placing rows and rows of the same item together in a display. Instead, arrange your showcase display with a variety of individual products The buyer can see each item clearly, examine it and check its price. This is enough information to make a decision in most cases. Be sure to watch the people in the store so you can offer help and additional information as needed.

Add an Unrelated Item

An item that is not related to the product you are selling draws the customer's eye to the products in the display. The item can be a holiday-themed knickknack or a stuffed animal, for example. If you choose an item that is interesting enough, customers might cross the room just to get a closer look at it. And, while they are there, they also get a closer look at the merchandise in the display.

Add Signs

Place signs around your store. Use short, clear phrases. Use the signs to promote special offers and discounts. Keep the signs fairly small and very tasteful. The signs will attract attention and guide customers to the products that interest them.

However, do not use so many signs that your store looks cluttered. E-cig customers, especially those willing to buy your best items, are more sophisticated than many other consumers. They have taken the time to learn about cutting edge technology and the newest types of pleasure to be found. They are not impressed by a hodgepodge of mismatched signs.

Move Sale Items to the Back
Customers do not mind making a little extra effort to find discounts. Put your sale items in the back or in another out of the way location in your store. Regular customers will look for them. When new customers find them, they get excited about your store. They have made an exciting discovery, and they want to tell their friends about it.

Change Displays Often
A good rule of thumb is to change your displays at least once a month. If you have new products coming into your store on a regular basis, you might want to change them every two weeks instead. Remember to keep the newest items closest to the front of the store and the oldest items toward the back.

Get Customer Opinions
As you talk to customers, ask them questions about the displays. For example, ask the customer which display she likes best. Ask her if she found everything she was looking for in your store. If several people have trouble finding a certain item, you can move that item to a more prominent location or dress up the display to attract more attention.

You can also ask the e-cig store customer these questions in the form of a survey. Give your customer a paper survey form along with any product information sheet you hand them. Place the survey sheets on the counter where they go to make their purchases. Or, you can do a phone survey. Set up your cash register to print a phone number and request for a survey. Use all these opinions for guidance in setting up your displays.

Know Your Hottest Selling Products

Study the data from your inventory to assess which products are selling better than others. If you find a product that is not selling well, think about whether or not it should be more popular than it is in your store. If you have an item that is well-liked among e-cig users but is not doing well, move that product to be sure people find it.

Your hottest selling products are likely already in prominent locations. Look at the profit margin on those items. If they are not making you any money, consider moving them to make way for products that are under-performing.

Step 6: Grand Opening

You are ready to open your doors for the first time. You have placed your advertisements in the local media, handed out flyers and given away promotional products. Now you have the opportunity to make a lasting impression on the e-cig users of the area. Your big day is here. It is time to focus on making your grand opening a monumental success.

Greet Every Customer at the Door

Every person who walks through your doors on grand opening day should get a special greeting. Let them know they are welcomed with open arms and that you care about them and their needs. Always smile, no matter how hectic the day becomes.

You have many duties for grand opening day, so get some help with the greetings. Even if you plan to run the store without additional counter help, you might need extra people that first day. Hire at least one person to help with the greeting and other opening tasks or enlist family members for the day.

Give Out Goodies

When people walk in the door, hand them something to remember you by. Give them a decorative bag containing your promotional materials such as flyers, brochures and a business card. Add a coupon for a free or discounted product on their next visit.

Finally, give them something they can use right away. Choose an item that is inexpensive for you but still valuable for the customer. Think of what they might be doing while they are using their e-cig, and give them a small item for that activity. For example, you can give away single serving gourmet coffee packets to drink when they vape in the morning. Be aware that, at the time of this writing, the FDA has stated that businesses cannot give out free samples of e-juice.

Team up with local merchants who sell related products and give them the opportunity to contribute to the goodie bag. To do this, you will have to allow them to promote their business by putting their logo on their sample or coupon. However, merchants who sell products related to vaping but do not sell e-cigs are great allies to have on your side.

Call a local radio station and tell them you are giving away t-shirts or other wearable advertisements to everyone who walks in your door and tells you they heard your advertisement on the radio. Or, you can make it even more fun by having them say a code word that you only give out on the air.

Provide Entertainment

Entertainment adds to the party atmosphere of your grand opening. You could pay a huge fee for a singer or comedian to perform if you have the funds. Or, if you are more interested in cutting costs and making more initial profit, you can find less expensive ways to entertain your opening day crowd. Hire a local band or simply create a soundtrack of pleasant music for your event. Remember to cater to local tastes in music, and choose music that appeals to the 30- to 50-year-old age group.

Introduce Your Products

Mingle with the crowd and show them what you offer in your store. Point out great deals and unique products. Talk to visitors about the types of e-juice and e-cigarettes you offer. Let them ask questions and give them specific answers. Some of the people who attend your grand opening may be trying out the idea of using an e-cigarette for the first time. Give them your full attention during the conversation and let them know you care about their needs.

Offer Information Packets

E-cigarettes are relatively new to the marketplace. Some customers might want more detailed information than you can possibly supply verbally during a grand opening. Give them handouts about e-cigs in general and about your products in particular. Ideally, you can make up information packets ahead of time that contain all these fact sheets.

Step 7: Operating Your Store

Your grand opening has concluded. It is time to think of daily operations. The next step discusses how to operate your store. Remember you will need to have this information and get everything ready to run your store on opening day.

Many customers will come to your grand opening ready to make a purchase. You have to have your cash registers, computer hardware and software. and inventory management system in place before that day arrives. You also need to be prepared for any problems or issues that might arise. Here is my advice on operating your store.

Choosing Cash Registers

Depending on your budget, you can get a simple cash register or a high-end register with POS and inventory management. Within our $20,000 budget, you have enough money to get a register that has many helpful features. Here are some facts to consider as you are choosing your cash register:

- Size Matters

  The size of your store and inventory make a big difference in how much you should spend on a cash register. For our moderately-sized store, you need a cash register that has enough features to help you with some of the tasks of running your store.

- Budget Counts

  Simple cash registers can run from $100 to $1000 and more advanced ones can run from $5000 to $20,000. Evaluate your budget to see what you can afford. Then, choose something within your price range. Obviously, you cannot get a $20,000 register if your total budget is $20,000, but you do not have to be satisfied with the cheapest model you find. Shop around for the best deal so you can have the most features possible within your budget.

- Security Is Essential

  In an e-cig store, you need to get out from behind the counter and mingle with the customers as much as possible. You need to be free to go to them and explain products or show them products they may have missed. Follow these tips for proper security.

  - Get a cash register with a locking drawer.
  - Have a small cash drop box.
  - Choose a cash register with a password protection feature.
- Inventory Tracking Is Optional

  If you have the funds and find a good enough deal, you can get a high-end cash register that tracks your inventory for you. However, if you do not have or do not want to spend the money, you can manage the inventory of an e-cig store with your PC.

- Receipt Printing Choices

  You need a cash register that provides a receipt, and there are two main options to consider. One is the thermal printer cash register that prints the receipt using heat. This is the more expensive register of the two, but there are fewer costs to keep it in service.

The other register type is the print ribbon cash register that requires you to buy toner cartridges. The advantage of this cash register is that it prints a receipt that is easier to read and does not fade away like the receipts made with a thermal printer.

- Who to Buy From

  You have the options of buying from a retailer or a cash register vendor. If you are buying one of the simpler models, an online or local retailer is the best choice in most cases. In fact, you can often find the less expensive models used online at sites like e-Bay or Craigslist. Or, you can look for a business that is closing up and offer to buy from them. However, if you are buying a more advanced model cash register, it makes sense to at least talk to a vendor and see what kind of deal they offer.

Choosing PC's

Computers play an important role in your business. You use them to shop for products and place orders. You can use them to track your inventory. When you need to generate a report, a PC makes the job monumentally easier than preparing it by hand.

You can keep customer information and order data on your PC, too. You can also communicate with customers, retail clients and suppliers using the email and messaging features on your computer. Your PC provides you easy access to media as well, which is important both for learning about your new industry and for submitting advertising and press releases to the media.

Computers provide an ideal way to manage your finances on a daily and monthly basis. What is more, you simply cannot run a website without a computer. This is important now, and will be even more crucial when you open your e-commerce site later.

So, what should you look for in a PC? The first consideration is how much computer you need now and in the foreseeable future.

As an e-cig retailer, you need a computer with a fast enough processor to allow you to use the Internet efficiently to view and order products, communicate with customers, and do the research necessary to keep your business on the cutting edge of the e-cig industry. Small business experts suggest that you need nothing less than dual core processors to run any business of any type.

You need more RAM than the average home user, but you do not need the same amount as a larger business would. Any business needs at least 4 gigabytes of RAM, and in today's technologically-advanced world, you can get much more and do much more with it.

You also need ample storage space to keep all your company data. A mid-range PC can provide this data storage easily. Memory is much cheaper than it used to be, so it costs very little to choose a computer with more memory. Experts suggest having about 250 to 500GB for a small business. Mid-range business computers are usually equipped within this range. If you find you need extra storage, you can always add an external hard drive. When you think about how much memory you need, remember to think "right-sized" rather than cheapest or top-of-the-line.

If it seems like a good idea to go to your local electronics outlet and buy the same computer you use at home, rethink that decision. Instead, choose a computer that is specifically designed for businesses. These computers stay operational more of the time, because they are easy to service and very durable.

You do not need fantastic graphics or audio for your business computer. An expensive graphics card is completely unnecessary for your e-cig business. After all, you will be working with alpha-numeric data most of the time. Never load games on your business computer. It is not only a waste of memory, but it can also make your PC unstable.

There are currently four main types of simple computer systems: desktop tower systems, all-in-one systems, net top systems and mini-PC's. Of these, your e-cig business runs best with either a tower or all-in-one desktop system.

Choosing Software

One more reason to avoid buying a cheap, consumer-type computer is to avoid the myriad of junk software that is loaded onto them. With a business computer, you avoid all this nonsense. The only trial offers you get are basic business programs like Microsoft Office. Choose it or not, at least you do not have to deal with a deluge of software offers popping up continually.

What software do you need for a business, then? Above everything else, you need word processing software and a spreadsheet program. Accounting software allows you to do your books with little or no help from an accountant. You can also choose software to track time if you have any employees besides yourself. In addition, you can get inventory-tracking software if your cash register does not have that function and you do not want to do it by hand.

Intuit's QuickBooks captures over 90% of the market for business accounting software. You can purchase the software for $200-$300 or use the online version for a small monthly fee. It is packed with customizable features, and the company provides excellent tech support. However, if you do not have any accounting experience, you probably need to invest in a QuickBooks class with a certified dealer to get the most out of the program.

QuickBooks is a good option in many cases, but it has more features than you are likely to need for your e-cigarette retail business. Another option is Sage. The Sage 50 version is downloadable software that runs just under $400 for one user, while the Sage One is less complex and works from the cloud at a monthly fee of about $25. The program is very accountant-friendly if you choose to go that route now or in the future. With Sage, it is even more important to know or learn something about accounting to use it.

If you want the capability of managing data in multiple currencies easily, Xero is another great option. Since foreign trade is almost always an important factor in the e-cig trade, Xero might be just right for your retail shop. One disadvantage of Xero is the lack of invoicing options. This might be a problem for you e-cig store, especially if you wholesale to other retailers.

So what is the right accounting software to buy? Make a list of the things you want to do with your accounting software. Then, shop these programs and others on the market to find the one that will do what you need it to do.

As far as word processing software, Microsoft Word is always a good choice. If you get Microsoft Office, you also have Excel spreadsheet, PowerPoint and the calendar, contacts and email features of Outlooks.

Keeping Track of Inventory

Inventory-tracking software allows you to keep current on what is selling and needs to be reordered as well as what is setting in your displays for months on end. If you choose QuickBooks for accounting software, you already have inventory management features built into the program. Or, you can use QuickBooks Plus Online for a monthly fee of about $40 if you do not use a barcode scanner.

To save even more money, you can do your inventory-tracking manually. However, the cost savings might not be worth the time you spend doing it. To track inventory without a computer program specifically intended to do it, you need to make a spreadsheet either on your computer or on paper.

Create a spreadsheet for your inventory. Start by naming the document and entering each of your products along the left hand side. Across the top, label columns for "original count," "expiration date," "date" and "remaining." After those four columns, continue by alternating the labels "date" and "remaining."

Now, write in everything that arrives on your first shipment. Remember to write the specific product along with its expiration date. Place price tags on each individual product in your inventory that include the same identifiers as you write down in your spreadsheet document. When a customer purchase the e-cigarette, e-juice or accessory, remove the label and set it aside.

To do inventory tracking, simply go through the stickers one by one. Mark down the number of each item sold under the "date" column. Subtract the number sold in your "date" column from the "original count" and write the result in the "remaining" column. Finally, as you repeat this process each day, subtract the number sold from the "remaining" number of the last day's business and enter it into the next "remaining" column. If you try this process and find that you are selling so much inventory that it is difficult to keep up, you can always switch to a software solution.

Setting Store Hours (mine are 10 to 7, 11 to 7 on Sunday)

When you set your store hours, always consider the activity patterns of your local area. When are people out shopping? Make sure to include those hours. My store hours are 10 a.m. to 7 p.m. Monday through Saturday and 11 a.m. to 7 p.m. on Sundays. This is the time people are moving around in the neighborhoods near my store and taking care of their shopping. These are generally the ideal hours for an e-cig business. However, if people in your community get up earlier or shop until later in the evening, change the hours to suit their needs.

Post-Opening Glitches and Issues:
After you have your grand opening and get down to daily business, you can expect to have some glitches and issues in your store. Take them in stride. They happen to everyone in every retail business. Have a plan in place for how to react to these minor setbacks.

- Returns

  Customers return products: it is a fact of life. Sometimes they have a good reason for doing so and sometimes they have simply changed their mind about the purchase. Your first job is to convey an attitude of helpfulness. Next, ask the customer why they are returning the product. Return the purchase price in all but cases where the customer is trying to defraud your store.

Then, determine whether or not the product can be reused. If it is unopened and still in its packaging, you can accept it and make a refund. However, if it was not sold in a package or has already been opened or sampled, you cannot resell it.

- Defective Products

  Eventually, you are bound to get a few defective products, even if you are dealing with a reputable supplier. Besides manufacturing problems, which should be few if you have chosen a reliable supplier, problems can happen during shipping. In any case, contact the manufacturer about the defective product. Read your contract or invoice for returns policies and work out a solution with your supplier.

- Customer Service

  Many people think customer service is all about handling complaints. However, if you practice good preventative customer service habits, you avoid these problems altogether. What do you do when a customer comes into your store and begins to look at your merchandise?

  First, you need to talk to them in a friendly way and encourage them to ask questions about your products. Ask if they have used an e-cigarette before and if so, what kind they used. If they are only familiar with disposable e-cigs, help them with instructions on how to use non-disposable ones. Tell them about how to change the cartridge and how to clean the e-cigarette. Talk to them about e-juice and how to use it. Show them accessories that improve their experiences with their e-cig.

If these practices fail and a customer comes to you with a complaint, hear them out. Get all the details before you come to any conclusions. Once you understand the issue, find the simplest, most amicable solution for both you and the customer. Always remember the value of repeat business and do everything you can reasonably do to satisfy your customer.

- Store Hours

  What if you find that your hours are not working for you or your customers? They are easily changed, but you need to be sure you can be open for people who want to purchase your products.

  If you decide to open earlier than the hours I suggested, do people come in during those morning hours? If not, consider opening later. By cutting down operating hours when there is no business, you can possibly stay open later to get any business you have been missing in the evening.

- Daily Promotion

  Always have a daily promotion. It keeps customers coming into the store regularly to see what is new. Be ready to tell customers about the promotion every day and answer any questions they have. Put up posters to let people know what the daily offering is and how they can take advantage of it.

- Customer Requests

  Customers who are more familiar with vaping often have specific products in mind when they visit a retail e-cig store. If you do not have these products on hand, you have two choices. Either you can order the product immediately, or you can try to interest them in similar products first. Your conversation with the customer gives you the information you need to decide between the two options.

  Try to order any products your customer wants to have. Write down exactly what the customer wants. Ask her for her contact information so you can get back to her as soon as you work out the details. Check with your supplier to see if they can get those products, and then order them at once.

Step 8: Post-Opening Marketing

You always need to keep up with your marketing efforts, even after your grand opening. Ongoing marketing and frequent special promotions during the year ensure that you are going to have more new customers. In addition, your current customers will keep coming back faithfully because they know you are always going to have a special sale or event to keep them happy.

Work to grab and keep the attention of people who use or are interested in e-cigs. You can do this for your local store in a variety of ways.

- o New Flyers
- o A Newsletter
- o Coupons
- o Posters for New Products
- o Daily Promotions
- o Special Events

Calendar-Centered Promotions

Create promotions centered around holidays and life events. These dates on the calendar are each associated with certain images and activities. Key in on what the customer is doing and thinking at these important times and find a way to relate it to e-cigs.

December Holidays

December is a happy time for most people. It is holiday time in many different cultures. People want to experience pleasure and share it with others. One of the best times to promote your e-cig line is while everyone is out shopping and taking more time off to relax and enjoy the holidays.

Here are some facts about recent holiday spending:

- • People coming to a sales promotion during the holidays expect at least a 30% discount.
- • Your target market, 30- to 50-year-olds, spend the most during the Christmas season.

- About 65% of consumers investigate products online before shopping in a local store.
- Shoppers love to hold the product in their hands and see it up close. In fact, that is one of the biggest reasons people shop locally.
- Shoppers love to get the best deal. For people who look online first, the fact that they are not paying extra for shipping is a big plus.

Seasonal Promotions

What do summer, fall, winter and spring all have in common? If you said they are all seasons to enjoy an e-cig, you guessed well. Promote the products in your line that are natural winners for the season at hand. People think of the beach in the summer, so feature e-juices that include tropical flavors. In fall, the crisp cool air is invigorating and reminds people of getting back to work after vacation. Fall is a great time to promote the more intense flavors of e-juice, or focus on getting your customer equipped with the right e-cigarette accessories.

Winter can be an exciting time of year, with all the holiday celebrations. It can just as easily be depressing. Concentrate your advertising on presenting upbeat images of home and relaxation. In spring, it is a time to begin anew. It is a great time to introduce your customers to the latest e-cig technology and e-juice flavors.

Email Marketing

Ask if your customer would like to get updates on new products and notices of sales from your store. If so, request their email address so you can send them your latest e-cig store news. Build a spreadsheet or database with the names and contact information of all your customers. Be sure this information is safeguarded to protect your customers' privacy.

Once you have your email list, you can begin crafting emails to send out periodically. Remember that no one likes to receive an excessive amount of email, even from a store they like. If you send out too many emails, your customers will eventually mark them as spam. Yet if you send out too few emails, you miss out on opportunities to reach out to them. Email once a week and you will find it is sufficient for keeping in touch with the people who have expressed interest in your store.

Step 9: How to Wholesale to Other Local Retailers

Now that you have opened your store and it is doing well, you can expand your business by working with local retailers. You provide a basic line of e-cigarette products at wholesale prices to a local business owner who then sells them at retail prices. This is a great way to limit your competition. Here are some simple steps you can take to get started.

Approach Gas Station Owners

Go to local gas station owners in the same town as your brick and mortar store or in a nearby town. Ask them if they would like to carry the e-cig to get back some of the business they have lost as people quit smoking as much. Explain that vaping is a new alternative to smoking. Quote them some statistics about how fast the market is growing and the kinds of profit they can make by joining you in this venture. Other businesses to approach include smoke-free hotels and restaurants.

Offer to Supply Basic E-Cig Line

Let the business owner know that they are not going to have to keep up with a large variety of merchandise. You will provide a basic e-cigarette line that appeals to the customers of their gas station or other retail store. Bring samples of your product so the business owner can look them over and try the product if he wants to do so before he decides whether or not to sell them.

Provide Promotional Materials

Before the business owner starts selling the e-cig line, bring him promotional materials to hand out to his customers. These materials, such as flyers, pamphlets and stickers to place on bags, can focus on the advantages of e-cigarettes over combustible cigarettes. In addition, you can provide your own store information on the promotional materials with images and/or descriptions of all your products. Include products from the full line of e-cigs, accessories and supplies you sell in your store.

Get There First

Good timing is essential as you approach other retailers. Get there first before others who want to sell e-cigarettes as much as you do. If you wait too long, you will have competition for this product that appeals most to a select group of people. Sometimes, all a retailer is waiting for is someone to offer the product. Make sure that someone is you and not someone else.

Part Two: Opening the e-Commerce Store

Once your business is in operation, you have the hang of it, and you are starting to make daily sales, you can relax a bit. At this point, you can start thinking about how to expand your business online and reach the whole world.

An online store has the potential of making you even higher profits than your brick and mortar store. You have very little overhead. There is no building to lease, no utilities to pay, and you avoid many other costs of doing business locally. The e-commerce store you set up can be much more cost-effective, so the income is significantly higher than in the actual retail store.

Here are the steps to opening your e-commerce store:

Step 1: Domain Registration and e-Commerce Hosting

Before you can open your e-commerce store, you first have to register a domain and set up e-commerce hosting. The set-up is not difficult, especially if you are reasonably Internet-savvy. Following are my thoughts on accomplishing these two tasks.

Domain Registration

Domain registration is purchasing and claiming a domain name that you can use in your URL's. In other words, when you register your domain, you are buying the basis for your web address. For best results, choose a domain name that follows these guidelines.

- It is easy to remember

- It includes keywords related to your business, such as e-cig, e-cigarette, e-juice or vape.
- It describes your company

Start by brainstorming for awhile to come up with several viable domain names. Think of what your potential customers might search for when looking for the products you sell. When you have a list of at least 10 names, go to a domain registration site and see if any of the domain names you have come up with are available. If several of your possible domain names are available, you can choose the one that you like best. Here is a list of the most popular domain name registration sites.

- Bluehost – Currently the most popular domain registrant, Bluehost offers domains for as little as $9.99 per year. You can choose from any or all of the following suffixes: .com, .net, .us, .bus, .info, .org, .name, .ws, .tv, .co.uk, and more. Bluehost offers many website services, but since you are creating an e-commerce site, what you really need from Bluehost is just the domain name. Once you purchase it, it goes with you to your chosen web host.
- Register.com – A very popular and long-standing domain registrar, this site offers a domain name along with a corresponding email address for about $40 per year.
- 1 & 1 Internet – This registrant is actually a web-hosting company that also sells domain names. Here, you can get a .com for as little as $6.99 per year.
- Dotster.com – Domain names at Dotster are around $15 for a .com domain name at the time of

this writing. Dotster offers a variety of domain services.

- NameCheap – At NameCheap, you get a domain name plus email forwarding for about $11 per month. Not bad, but just slightly higher than GoDaddy.
- Bigcommerce – In the next section, I offer suggestions for e-commerce hosting. If you choose Bigcommerce for your e-commerce hosting, you can get a domain name from them directly rather than transferring a domain name from another registrar.

e-Commerce Hosting

Once you have nailed down your domain name, the next step is to set up your e-commerce store. For that, you need an e-commerce host. There are many e-commerce hosts to choose, but I will limit my recommendations to what I consider the top three.

Bigcommerce

Bigcommerce is my top pick for e-commerce solutions. This e-commerce host offers a tremendous array of services for you e-commerce site. At Bigcommerce, you can offer 100 individual products for $15 per month or as many as a thousand for $35 per month. The web host gives you unlimited storage with no transaction fees.

With their e-commerce site store-builder, Bigcommerce makes it easy for you to input all your products, add photos and prices, and generally run your e-commerce store. They provide services to allow you to process payments by credit cards, PayPal and Google Payments. Bigcommerce also makes it simple to handle payments in foreign currencies. In addition, the web host helps you manage tasks like returns and recurring payments.

Bigcommerce is a Google Partner, meaning that they have staff members that have passed the Google AdWords certification exams. The Partners designation also indicates that they have a proven track record for handling their clients AdWords Pay-Per-Click campaigns very well.

You do not have to worry about what to charge for tax when you use Bigcommerce. They keep their system up-to-date with all the most current tax rates and calculates the tax for you. Your e-commerce site and your customers' information stay safe with Bigcommerce's SSL security features.

Shopify

Shopify is another e-commerce web host. They offer over 100 e-commerce website templates. Their focus, in fact, is on building high quality sites. If you choose their mid-range service, it costs $79. That includes 5GB of storage, unlimited products, a discount code engine, abandoned cart recovery, gift cards and a mobile app feature, all with no transaction fees.

Shopping Cart Elite

Shopping Cart Elite focuses on the shopping cart software. They also provide cloud hosting for your e-commerce site. This provider offers integration with Amazon in addition to your on-site product displays and customer purchase features. They offer a full range of management solutions for your e-commerce site, including customer, tax, order, discount, shipping, inventory, employee and supplier management.

After you choose and register your domain name and select an e-commerce web host, you are ready to build your site. Most shopping cart software services are fairly easy to follow as you set up your e-commerce store. Be sure to contact their customer support team if you have any questions about how to build your website. In my business experiences, Volusion has proven to offer excellent help in getting the site ready to go.

Step 2: Finding a CC Processor

CC Processor stand for credit card processor. This is the service that makes it possible for you to accept payment by credit card online. A reliable credit card processor not only performs the transactions, but also quickly approves or disapproves payment and keeps your customers' card data safe.

Choosing a CC Processor is an important task to complete as you set up your e-commerce store. Research the CC Processor providers carefully and compare what they offer. To help you with this job, here are my recommendations.

Flagship Merchant Services

Flagship is perhaps the most popular of the e-merchant services available. They process all major credit cards, authorize payments directly from the customer's account, and accept payments from customers around the globe. They offer excellent fraud prevention features that protect both you and your customer. The only real disadvantage to Flagship is for merchants who run their businesses from somewhere other than the U.S. The services are simply not available for any other source location.

CreditCardProcessing.com

This service is very similar to Flagship Merchant Services. While you can only operate from the U.S., you can accept credit cards from international customers. In addition, they offer a free mobile app so customers can complete transactions on the go. CreditCardProcessing.com offers a "lowest rate guarantee," but you can only take advantage of it after you have already worked with another CC Processor first.

Volusion

Along with all their other e-commerce solutions, Volusion provides excellent CC Processing. Submit your application to Volusion, or to any CC Processor, early so you are ready to accept credit cards before you launch your e-commerce site.

Leaders

Leaders offers CC Processing at low rates. They have a simple set-up procedure, and also accept payments from mobile devices. The only problem with Leaders is that those low rates do not always apply to debit cards from the smaller banks. However, all in all, it is an affordable and reliable e-commerce CC Processing service.

Since e-cig e-stores are a global business, I want to mention some payment processors based outside the U.S. Authorize.net provides reliable and secure payment processing in Europe. For Canada e-stores, I recommend BeanStream. SecurePay provides these services for e-stores based in and around Australia.

Step 3: Building Your e-Store

Everything is ready at this point to start doing business online – except you still need to build your e-cig store and merchandise it. As you build your e-commerce store, ask for help from your e-commerce web hosting customer support center whenever necessary. However, you can do most of the work unaided by following these simple steps.

How to Build the e-Store

Templates

You are ready to build your site. Once you choose an e-commerce hosting service, you can choose an e-commerce website template from their catalog. In most cases, if you choose a free template, others may use it as well. If you choose to pay for a premium template, read the conditions carefully to know whether others can use that template or not.

Even if other websites have the same basic template as you do, you will still have a unique site depending on how you customize it. You add your own Home Page image and business logo to the template. Input your company information so that it shows up on every page of your site.

Organize

The next step is to organize your store. Create categories of products. For your e-cig e-store, you might use columns like e-cigarettes, e-cig accessories, e-cig kits and e-liquid. Then, break your list down to a second level of categories to enhance site navigation. For the category of e-liquid, for example, you might have standard tobacco flavors, premium tobacco flavors, tropical flavors, etc.

Products

After you have made the categories to organize your store, start stocking your virtual shelves. For each item, just input the name, code, price and weight of the product. Enter a product description. Write your own description if possible, to get better results on search engines. Click Save and go on to the next product.

Payment Processing

Set up your payment processing next. In the Admin section, enter your payment credentials for the CC Processor you have chosen. Enter your country, then the CC Processor Gateway, and finally, the CC Processor's API ID and transaction key. Select the credit and debit cards you want to accept.

Tax Rate

Prepare your site to charge tax. In most cases, it is a simple matter of entering your location (your state abbreviation and name spelled out). Then, you add the tax rate based on current government rules.

Shipping

Define shipping parameters. Mark the shipping to country field so that the countries you want to ship to are highlighted and the ones you do not want to ship to are not. In the shipping to field, mark where your shipments will come from – either directly from your site or from a supplier's site. Finally, choose the shipping carrier you want to use for each state and country.

Other Pages

In addition to your Home Page and Product Pages, you need the following pages for your site: About Us, Terms and Returns, FAQ. An optional page for clearance items and/or new items brings customers back to your store again and again.

Meeting Basic e-Commerce Site Requirements

In the sections above, I have explained most of the basic e-commerce site requirements. Here is a list for your reference:

- Domain Name
- E-Commerce Web Hosting and Software

- CC Processor
- SSL Certificate

   The SSL Certificate assures customers that their information, including credit card and bank information, is safe when they buy products at your site. SSL stands for secure socket layer. SSL encrypts your customers' personal information as it is transferred through the CC Processor for payment. You can often get an SSL Certificate through your e-commerce hosting site. Request this service early because it takes at least 7 to 10 days for installation.

Hiring a Virtual Assistant

A virtual assistant is like an administrative assistant for you e-store. A virtual assistant can actually help you with business tasks in both your offline and online stores. At both stores, the VA can do word processing, answer phone calls and do other tasks for smooth operation of your business. However, with an e-store, you absolutely must have someone to take customer service calls, preferably 24/7.

Find a company that offers VA services or post a job on a job board. Communicate clearly about what you expect the VA to do, what hours you want them to work, how much you will pay, and any other details about how you want the job to be done.

Hiring a virtual assistant is easy, but you need to be just as ready to fire a VA if they are not doing their job. Monitor their performance and reevaluate their continued employment periodically.

Step 4: Merchandising Your e-Store

Just as you did with your bricks and mortar store, you need to merchandise your e-store for maximum effect and profit. Here are some tips that are effective for online merchandising.

Featured Items

Set up a "featured items" section, preferably on your home page. Use this section to show off new products or items with a high ROI. Change the featured item as often as possible to keep your site fresh and your customers interested.

Similar or Related Products

When a customer clicks on one of your products, let them see products that are similar but less expensive when you want to get rid of excess stock or push a certain product. You can also show similar but more expensive products to interest your customer in spending more on your site. Another tactic is to show related products that the customer needs when they order the item. For example, if the customer has clicked on a particular e-cigarette, display accessories and e-liquids. Add clickable links so the customer can move quickly to that other product.

Site Search

Offer a site search feature if your e-commerce web software has the capability. This makes it much easier for customers to find what they want if they already have a specific item in mind.

If you have followed my instructions so far, you are all ready to open up your e-store. And, with the website set up properly, all you have to do is click the button to go live. But just because your site is live, that does not mean that anyone can find your e-commerce site on the web.

Certainly it is time to open your e-store, but once you do that, you need to focus on getting the word out that it is there.

Step 5: Opening Your e-Store

Create an online opening event. In internet terms, this is called launching your e-commerce site. The best way to launch your site is to use the full power of the Internet by putting out press releases and news flashes, and by using the proper techniques to rank high on search engine results pages. Following is a brief explanation of how to let people know you are open for business.

Press Releases

Press releases help you get the word out that you are opening an e-cigarette store. People find them online by searching for them, or read them in the newspaper and other media sources. You can also add them to your website so customers can keep up with the latest news on your company.

If you have good language skills, you can write PR's yourself. Even if not, you can still use these hints to check the work of any copywriter you hire to write your press releases.

- Grab Their Attention

  Have an opening paragraph that grabs the reader's attention. Use statistics about the e-cig industry or little known facts about e-cigs. Along with the "hook" in the opening paragraph, you need to include enough information to let the reader know what the PR is going to be about as you continue.

- News Angle

Any press release needs a news angle. In fact, many sources will not accept a PR without one. The news, in this case, is your grand opening. Later on, you can put out press releases whenever you like, as long as they are framed in the form of a news article. Of course, you want the news to be positive in most cases.

- Answer the 5 basic questions of news: who, what, when, where and how.

- Use Quotes

  Use quotes to lend a personal touch to the press release and help people identify with the news they find there. If you are writing the press release yourself, add something you want to say or a direct quote from an industry source. Be sure to credit the source. If someone else is writing your press release, give them a quote to use as a part of the assignment.

- Call to Action

  A call to action tells people what to do after they read the press release. It might be a request to visit your store or website. Another option is to tell the readers they can follow a link to a coupon.

- Distribute Press Releases

  Online press release distribution is fairly easy once you find the sites to do it. There are several sites that feature press releases, and you can find them through search. Look for sites that are specialized for the e-cig industry or related products and services.

For an offline press release, it is best to request guidelines from the news outlet before you write or make the assignment to write. Every newspaper has its own rules about what you can say and how you can say it, so save time and ask first. Sometimes you can find this information on the news outlet's website.

- Hiring a PR Writer

You want the best possible press release to introduce your company to the world. If writing is not your specialty, think about hiring someone who knows exactly how to do it.

Before you hire a copywriter to craft your grand opening press release, ask plenty of questions. How long have they been in business? How many press releases have they written? How did they learn to write PR's? Then, ask for a sample press release and check it against the hints in this guide.

Grand Opening News Flashes

You have probably heard the term "news flash" used in a variety of ways. Newscasters may say it or display it on a screen. Radio announcers also use the term. Young people may even say it in a sarcastic way to indicate that what someone said is not anything new.

In the business world, a news flash is a short, emphatic message to potential customers. It is similar to a press release, but it is usually shorter and has a headline that is hard to ignore. News flashes are like "breaking news" in that there is urgency in the message.

Here are some tips for writing or evaluating news flashes:

- Strong headline
  - Use words like "Breaking," "Flash," "Bulletin," "Newsbreak," or "Update."
  - Bold it, use a bright color like red, add a graphic to make it stand out.
    - Make it informative.
  - Dense Body
    - The body of the newsflash needs to be packed with information.
    - There should be no words that do not serve the purpose of promoting your Grand Opening.

A Grand Opening newsflash, just like a press release, should tell the most important facts in the first paragraph. These facts include:

  - The name of your store
  - Your store is having a grand opening
  - What you sell
  - Which City or Town your store is in
  - When the Grand Opening will be

In the rest of the newsflash, continue with more dense information such as:

- Grand Opening Specials
- Exact address and driving directions
- Store Hours
- A Call to Action (use a clickable link whenever possible)

Distribute the Grand Opening newsflash widely in your area and online. You can send them out to these media outlets:

- Popular E-Cig Blogs
- E-Cig Forums like ECF
- Press Release Sites
- Your Facebook Page (include a link to your site)
- Twitter (a shortened version with a link to your site)

Step 6: Promoting Your e-Store

Promoting your e-store is somewhat different that promoting your brick and mortar store. You reach out to local customers with promotions that appear in the local media. However, to reach the world, you have to think differently. You have to appeal to a broader range of people and help them find you through the search engines. Here are some tips to help you do just that.

How to Rank on Search Engines

You can learn a great deal about search engines very quickly. It is all about Search Engine Optimization (SEO). Although the algorithms that rule the search engines change fairly frequently, some concepts have been around quite awhile and will likely continue to be important.

- Keywords and Keyword Phrases

Keywords are words that relate to your business in such a way that people will search for them on Google, Yahoo, Bing or other search engines. Keyword phrases are even better for search because they help you find your target market and appeal to the specific needs of your customers.

- Choosing Keyword Terms

    As you choose the keyword terms for your website, imagine you are someone looking to buy an e-cig or e-cig accessory. How would you look for it? What would you type into the search bar?

    Make your keywords as specific as possible. For example, one keyword might be e-juice. To make it more specific and appeal to a specific crowd, use a phrase like "chocolate e-juice" or "cheap e-juice." Brand names can also be a part of a keyword phrase.

    You can list your keywords in the meta data on your website. However, this practice has become less important as the Internet has evolved. The most important thing about keywords is that you use them in your promotional PR's, blog posts and website to direct customers to your site.

    One more thing about keywords: Avoid keyword stuffing. In the old days of search, SEO writers would write the same keyword over and over on each page of a site. The old algorithms picked up the references and placed the sites high on their search engine results page. Some SEO writers actually put the unrelated keywords on the site in such a way that they were invisible to the consumer. That practice is a part of black hat SEO, to be avoided at all cost.

Times have changed. Now, you simply need to say the keyword 2 or 3 times per page, and then use a few synonyms and related keywords. Using too many keywords on a page too much of the time will send your site plummeting closer and closer to the end of the results for that search term. Google neither looks kindly on keyword stuffing nor rewards it in any way. In fact, if it is too excessive, they punish it.

- Meta Tags

Meta tags consist of information about your website. They can include who wrote the website, when it is updated, and other information pertinent to your site. They are written in HTML and do not show on your site when customers visit your e-commerce store Instead, they are more to help the search engines index your site.

- Meta Descriptions

As you build your e-commerce site, look for the meta information tab. There is a field for meta description there. The meta description shows on the search engine under the heading or name of your site. This description should include what your site sells (e-cigs) and should hook the reader into clicking on your link. Remember that search engines generally lop off any part of the meta description that surpasses 160 characters in length.

- Tag Product Images

    Your e-commerce site needs to show images of everything you sell. To make these images show up on search, you need to add HTML tags to them. When you upload the images to your site, there should be a place to add your tag there. The tag should describe the picture as clearly as possible using a short phrase with one or two keywords.

- Relevance

    As of this writing, the most important thing to remember about website and other online content for your e-cig store is that the keywords and tags need to be relevant to the landing page of your site. The landing page is the Home page or any page you link to in an advertisement, article or blog post. Thus, it does not help you to use a keyword that is unrelated to your site, even if it is a popular keyword. Reveal who you are and what you sell through the meta data, and the search engines reward you with higher SERP's.

- Unique Content

    As much as possible, use your own unique content on your site and on any blogs or press releases you create to link to the site. Content that is copied and pasted from other sites ranks poorly on Google Search and other search engines.

- Inbound Links

Google considers how many people are linking to your website when calculating your Page Rank. The very best way to get inbound links is to follow the advice above on providing relevant content on your website. Another way to get these links is to write guest posts for popular blogs. The blogger allows you to provide a link to your site, and voila! You have created another inbound link.

Become a Social Media Expert

Social media sites like Facebook and Twitter represent one of the most significant ways to connect with your e-commerce site target market. The sites are gaining popularity with the adults in your target group. Harness the power of social media and your business prospects increase dramatically.

Set up a Facebook Page and a Twitter account. To gain followers on Twitter, search Trending Topics for e-cig keywords. Then, follow people who are talking about your products and industry. Most times, people will follow you back. You can also put social media buttons on your website so that people who visit it can connect with you.

You can add Facebook fans quickly by running an inexpensive Facebook Ad. First, write an informational post that includes the link to your Facebook Page. Ask people to Like your page. Then, click on "Boost Post" and create your Facebook Ad. Choose keywords related to your e-commerce business and select the amount you want to spend to promote your post. This can be very inexpensive. I did one of these ads to reach over 1000 people in 1 day, and it only cost me $15. You determine the budget for the Ad when you set it up. You can see the number of people the post is projected to reach. Adjust the keywords and amount until you get the results you like before you purchase the Ad.

Once you have followers, interact with them regularly. Authority is the name of the game in social media. Establish a reputation as an expert on e-cigarettes and related supplies. Offer advice on vaping issues and the best e-cig products to buy. Give customer service help to your e-cig customers. Whatever you do, avoid a selling tone and concentrate on establishing relationships with e-cig users.

Put Out Coupon Codes

Coupon codes are very popular among Internet users. They look for coupon codes for their favorite products. Potential customers use coupon codes when they stumble across them and want to try your products. Look for sites that frequently offer coupon codes and post your codes there. Here are two of my favorites.

- E-Cigarette Forums

  E-cig forums provide an ideal place to distribute your coupon codes on the Internet to customers and future customers around the world. People go to these forums to talk to others who like to vape. They get tips on making e-juice and filling their cartridge, for example. They also go for opinions on what are the best e-cigarettes on the market. While they are there, they keep an eye out for e-cig coupons. The forum I like best for this is the ECF forum found at http://www.e-cigarette-forum.com/forum.

  As I mentioned earlier in this guide, people often choose local stores because they want to avoid shipping costs. One of the best coupons out there is free shipping. Forum users are savvy online shoppers. However, they might be enticed to buy e-cigs locally to avoid these costs. A coupon for free delivery to their address can change their minds and get them interested in shopping at your e-commerce site.

- Groupon

Groupon is a specific site for coupons and coupon codes. It works like this: You place an ad with groupon that includes some kind of discount or coupon code. You only pay for the ad if the required number of customers respond and accept the offer.

People who want to take advantage of the offer often email, message or even call others who think might be interested in the Groupon offer. The reason the try to get others on board is because the offer is only good if enough people use it.

The result is usually that you get a flood of orders from people who want to use the coupon code or discount. In one case, a cupcake shop used a Groupon promotion and got so much business they had to provide over a hundred rain checks so people could come back and use the code.

Get people to move freely from your site to your store and vice versa. You can accomplish cross promotion by offering discounts, giving directions or URL's and location-based SEO. You can also get great results by cross promoting with other e-cig store that offer related but different products to your own.

- Discounts

  Offer your online customers a discount if they drop into the offline store. You can do this by enticing people to sign up for a newsletter. Then, you send out coupons to their email address that they can print out and bring to the store.

  In the same way, you can send out flyers containing coupon codes for the online store or add a coupon code to the sales receipt. Of course, you need to let them know the URL of your site so they can find it to use the code.

- URL's and Local Directions

  To direct offline customers to your online store, give them a card with the URL of your e-commerce site. You can also place this information on plastic bags you use to wrap the products after sale. You can even make up t-shirts, hats and other promotional products with a catchy slogan on the front and the URL for your site across the back. Not only will your customers have a way of remembering your domain name, but others see it as well.

The simplest way to send online customers to your brick and mortar store is to provide a map and driving directions right on your e-commerce site. Be sure to have a link from your home page to this directions page so it is easy to find once customers are on your site.

- Location-Based SEO

Location-based SEO is the hottest thing in niche marketing right now. You simply add a keyword describing your location, such as your state or town, into a keyword phrase containing your product. Use this keyword phrase on your Home page if possible, as well as on the About page and the Directions page.

- Cross Promotion with Other Businesses

Cross promotions are not limited to your own business. You can cross promote with businesses that are related to you. A classic example is a hotel that promotes local tourist attractions on their site. Since you are selling e-cigarettes, accessories and supplies, you need to find another business which appeals to the same people who use these supplies.

The Last Word

If you have made it this far, you now know how to get started in the e-cigarette retail business. You know how to open a brick and mortar store and an e-commerce site. You are ready to do business locally and enjoy a booming global business.

E-cigarettes, e-cig accessories and e-juice are in extremely high demand right now. The interest in and popularity of the product is predicted to grow very quickly for decades into the future.

Now that you know what the e-cigarette business is all about, are you ready to get started? Then, get onboard today! Visit my website to learn even more. Try different e-cigarettes and e-juices. Form your own opinions. Research the industry and learn more about the topics I have discussed.

You are on your way to a very profitable future. Get started now. The profits are right around the corner!

Appendix 1A: List of Reputable e-Cigarette Manufacturers

When you are just starting out in the e-cigarette retail business, choosing products can be confusing. To add to the problem, not all e-cig manufacturers put out quality merchandise. Below is a list of e-cigarette manufacturers who have proven to be trustworthy to deliver a high quality product. Here is the current list:

Joyetech

Innokin

Smoketech

Blu by Lorillard Tobacco

Kanger

China is the main supplier of e-cigarette devices, with over 1000 manufacturers in that country. Both the prices and the quality of these devices vary widely from manufacturer to manufacturer. Although I have supplied this short list of my favorite and most trusted manufacturers, there are plenty of other ones that produce high quality e-cigarette lines.

Some of the smallest manufacturers also make some fantastic products as well. My advice is to use the trusted brands above and also experiment with other manufacturers (from Alibaba.com)to find the products you like best at reasonable prices. Once you have gone through this trial and error process, you can choose a few great ones to carry. Right now, I rely on just 3 companies for all my e-cigarette devices.

One thing to remember is that the e-cigarette business is growing and changing rapidly. If you keep up with the changes, you might change your source of products in as little as two months.

You can keep up with the latest trends by visiting my site for my current recommendations. Or, if you prefer, you can simply set up an account with any of the manufacturers listed above. Just be aware that these are major name brand companies, so their prices are generally a bit higher than those of smaller manufacturing companies.

I list the most current suppliers I am buying from on my e-cigarette site. To get the most recent update, visit my site at http://bestelectroniccigarettehq.com . There, you can find new updates as well as product and store promotion ideas for free.

Appendix 1B: E-Liquid Sources

Finding great e-liquid sources is much different and much more difficult than locating suppliers for e-cigarette devices. The first thing you need to know is to stay away from Chinese e-liquid providers. Their products are usually much cheaper, but here are two other considerations that, to me, are much more important.

Quality:

There are several problems with the quality of e-liquids made in China. The quality of the e-liquids from China manufacturers is not consistently high. The ingredients used by most China manufacturers are often substandard. They do not use USDA grade flavorings or the VG-PG blend. Also, the facilities where the ingredients are mixed are generally below reasonable standards.

Shipping Expense:

Shipping e-liquids from China is much different and more expensive than shipping e-cigarette hardware. One problem is that U.S. customs imposes a higher import duty on liquids than on devices. Even the carriers that deliver e-cigarette products charge more for the e-liquids than the hardware.

Exceptions to the Rule:

A few U.S. companies own manufacturing facilities in China and in Hong Kong because labor is cheaper there. When you buy from these companies, the e-liquid container might have a label that indicates it was made in China. But this is nothing to worry about as long as you know the company that owns the facility is a reputable U.S. company. They follow high standards and procedures, and they use USDA grade ingredients.

U.S. manufacturers of e-liquids tend to have very high standards and quality. The main issue to be aware of is that prices are generally higher for U.S. e-liquid. In some cases, the prices are too high to allow you the profit you need in your e-cigarette store. So, finding good local manufacturers who wholesale at a reasonably rate is a challenge.

Getting great e-liquid at reasonable wholesale prices is an important key to succeeding in this business. The reason is simple: people do not need new devices every week, but they will come back weekly for more e-juice. Sell great tasting e-liquid at a reasonable price, and you can be sure that customers will return again and again.

Points to Remember about e-Liquid for Resale

1) You need to carry all strengths of tobacco and menthol e-liquids, including 0mg, 6mg, 12mg, 18mg and 24 mg.
2) Tobacco is the number one seller, as long as you carry great tasting varieties.
3) Fruit flavors like Blueberry, Peach, Strawberry, Pomegranate, Grape, Watermelon and Mango are also popular.
4) You do not need every strength of every fruit flavor. Instead, buy a few 0mg of one or two flavors and a few 18mg; then choose 12mg for the rest of your fruit e-liquid flavors.
5) In addition to tobacco, menthol and fruit flavors, choose spice and drink flavors. Some examples of these are Vanilla, Cinnamon, Fire and Ice (cinnamon and menthol combined), Coffee, Cappuccino, Vanilla Cream and Latte. For these, the medium nicotine strength usually sells best.

6) The fourth type of e-liquid to consider buying is the new wave energy and mood altering flavors. I do not personally know anything about their effectiveness or how they work, but many people say they are the best e-liquids, so I carry them. The top seller of this type is the Energy mix that is similar to Red Bull. Some suppliers are now offering aphrodisiac e-liquids. Both of these e-liquid mixtures are growing fast, along with other similar ones.

7) Beware of suppliers that sell e-liquids with well-known name brands such as Marlboro or Red Bull. You are buying serious trouble when you choose e-liquids with these popular names. They are unlawful for you to sell.

8) Set limits on how much you will pay for e-liquids. A 10ml bottle should not cost more than $2.50, and a 30ml bottle should not cost more than $4.50. If you want to remain competitive with most e-liquid retailers, you need to be able to keep prices at $5.99 to $7.99 for the 10ml bottle and $9.99 to $13.99 for the 30ml bottle.

Check out my blog at http://bestelectroniccigarettehq.com and follow my links for an updated list of reputable e-liquid suppliers.

Appendix 2: Basic Standard Order Sheet Examples

Here are some tips for ordering e-cigarette supplies, as well as a sample order sheet I recently submitted to one of my manufacturers. This order sheet not only shows the types of products I order, but it also gives details about choices to make for each type of product.

In addition, you can see by looking at the order sheet the quantities of e-cig supplies you need to start your business. I started with 50 to 100 pieces at a time.

In your first order, make sure to choose some of each of the following items:

1) Basic Kits
2) Basic Atomizers
3) Basic Batteries
4) A few high-end batteries such as the ego C twist 1100mAh
5) Chargers, including both wall-type and USB-type.
6) Zip Cases for your custom kits you make up on demand. (Customers want kits with a Pro tank and a 1100mAh battery.)
7) Choose zip cases in 3 to 4 different colors so you can make different types of kits using different colors. This makes it much easier to quickly distinguish between, for example, a kit with a Pro Tank atomizer in one color zip case and a 1100 C twist battery in another color.

Here is the sample order form:

Item	Quantity	$/Unit	Price	Questions/Comments
			0	
1. Ego CE4 Single New Kit w/USB Charger	200		0	Mixed Color
2. e Smart Kit w/USB Charger	100		0	
3. Wax Vaporizer, Disposable	100		0	
4. Ego CE4 Kit in Zinc Case	50		0	
5. D3 Atomizer (Glass Wax Atomizer)	50		0	
6. JT H2 Atomizer	100		0	Mix and Match Color
7. Pro Tank Single Atomizer	20		0	
8. EvoD Atomizers	100		0	Black and Blue

9. CE4 with Pen Cap Atomizer	100		0	
10. Evod Battery 1100 mAh	50		0	Top 3 Colors
11. Ego Battery 1300 mAh	50		0	Top 4 Colors
12. Diamond Battery 650 mAh	50		0	Top 4 Colors
13. Ego Twist 1100 mAh	25		0	Top 3 Colors
14. Ego Battery 900 mAh	50		0	Top 3 Colors
15. Ego M Zipper Case	50		0	Blue, Red, Pink, Green, Purple, but No Black
16. Mask for 650 Battery	10		0	
17. New Ego Case	50		0	
18. 18650 Charger, U.S.	25		0	
19. 18650 Battery	25		0	
20. AMK	25		0	

Set				
21. Vamo Kit	10		0	
22. Car Charger	50		0	
23. Ego Sling with My Logo	100		0	
24. New Leather Fashion Lanyard	50		0	
25. Disposab le Rubber Tips	500		0	
26. Rubber Chuck	50		0	
27. Show Shelf #2 (Atomize r Rack)	20		0	
28. Show Shelf #4 (Battery Display Rack)	20		0	
29. Show Shelf #1 (Drip Tip Rack)	20		0	
30. Show Shelf #5 (E-Liquid Rack)	10		0	

31. WOW Set Sample	1		0	Sample
32. D2 Solid Glass Sample	5		0	Sample
Total:			0	

Notes:

See what you can do to offer me a lower price overall.

Also find out how much the shipping charges are for this.

Please find the best shipping rate possible.

Appendix 3: Sample Promotional Materials

Promotional materials are crucial for effective local marketing. You can make great flyers, handouts and other promotional materials. All you need to make them for free are some basic skills in using MS Publisher.

You can also hire someone to make the promotional materials for you. I usually use fiverr.com, where I pay approximately $5 to $10 for the service. When you use fiverr.com or other designers, you need to plan ahead. Allow at least 3 to 4 days to receive your order.

Here is my very first flyer. I designed it myself because I was short on time and needed to get the promo going as quickly as possible.

We Carry Full Line of Premium Electronic Cigarettes and Accessories

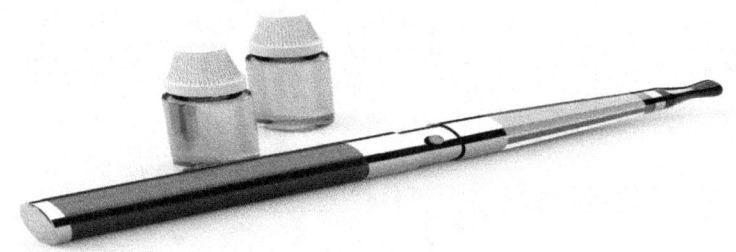

This Month's Special

Ego 650mAh Single in White Box with USB $19.99

Ego 650mAh Single Gift Case $22.99

EVOD Double Kit With Charger $ 45.99

10ml Premium Florida e-Liquid $6.99

Evod Atomizers $7.99

650 mAh Evod Battery $12.99

We also carry all types of Batteries, Atomizers, Wall Chargers and USB Chargers

Appendix 4: Basic Information Handouts to Customer

Many customers are new to e-cigarettes, and even those who have used them before can often benefit from more information. The best kinds of handouts to give customers have photos or illustrations and instructions on how to use and care for their e-cigarettes. Here is one I use in my e-cig retail store.

Simple Tricks and Tips on How to Use your new Device

1. How to Fill your Atomizer/Clearomizer with e Liquid?

Depending on the model you bought, these things canbe fileld either from the top or from the bottom. Typically Atomizers/Clearomizers like MT4, eVod or T series atomizers are filled from the bottom. Simply hold them upside down and gently unscrew the bottom base than fill liquid at an angle while making sure not to get any in the center hole. refer to the picture below.

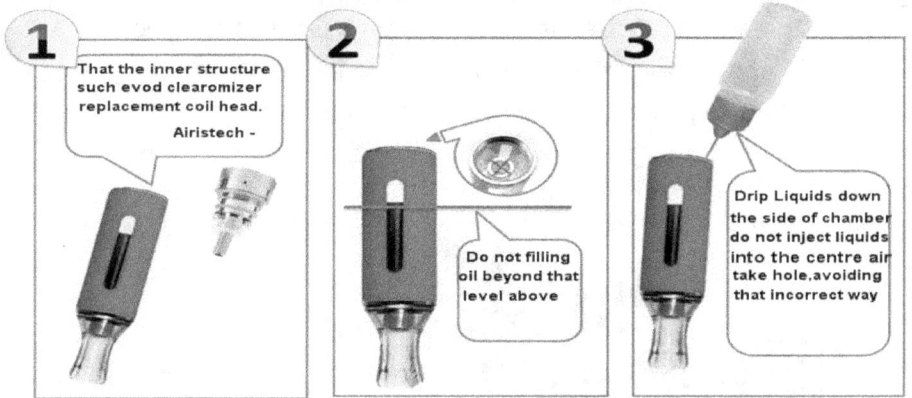

Typically CE4 type atomizers/Clearomizers are filed from the top, simply unscrew the mouth piece/drip tip and fill at an angle while making sure not to get any liquid on the center hole. See picture below

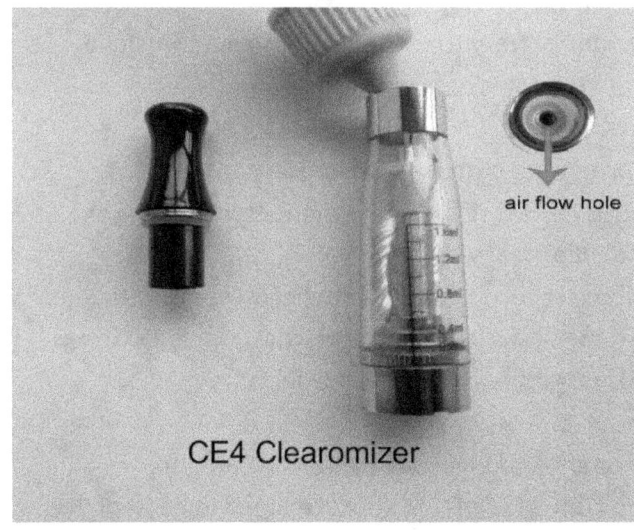

air flow hole

CE4 Clearomizer

2. How to Turn on the Battery?

Most Ego style battery comes standard with a safety switch. You may have to press and release the power button 5 times to turn it on. Similarly when not in use or you are carrying it around, you can press the same button 5 times to turn the battery off.

3. Basic Cleaning tips to make your device last longer:

- At every refill, take the atomizer off the battery, clean the battery terminal with a Q tips make sure no liquid is left inside the thread or outside.
- Before putting your battery to recharge, make sure to clean the battery every time.
- Do not drop your device.
- Only recharge when the battery is completely out of charge
- If your atomizer is leaking liquid on to the battery change the atomizer, do not vape leaky device.
- On any new Atomizer if you get dry vape, gently blow into the Atomizer so the wicks can soak than vape
- Change your Atomizers every two weeks for best vaping experience.
- If you experience constant leakage from atomizers, try changing your e Liquid type to a VG based liquid instead of PG based liquid, generally VG based e liquids are thicker and produce more smoke.

- If you are using Variable voltage batteries, start off with the lowest setting(3.2v) for any atomizers and see how it taste, than go up from there and find your sweet spot.